Lovely Life in Rhymes

Caroline Sands

BookLeaf Publishing

Presentation by *BookLeaf Publishing*

Web: www.bookleafpub.com

E-mail: info@bookleafpub.com

ISBN: 9789357440387

First edition 2023

DEDICATION

I want my sister to know that without you, my life would have been a complete nightmare before every Christmas.

From Coraline to Caroline again.

And i especially want to dedicate this book to my partner in life, love and happiness. My reason to smile. My heart sends each new words i have written since we met to you.

XO

(Can't spell careful without Care

Can't spell careless without care.)

ACKNOWLEDGEMENT

Again, i thank my parents for teaching me values and morals. My fifth grade teach Mrs. Dennessen for being such a kind and patient women. My role model as a student as far as a supportive and caring teacher. And i want to thank my sister for being my friend, my inspiration and my strength.

PREFACE

Life is a journey too glorious to hold onto your anger.
Our hate can be spelled out and thrown away and it would be better served.
The most of my poems are based on my imagination views of a happy and calm world where it is completely unreal to believe in a world where no one has any uncared for needs to simply live.
A simple view i can still never grasp the inevitable consequences that is forcing this never comes to reality.

To being the light i want the world to feel close each day.
The happiness of not having worries or added unnecessary responsibilities.

Ahh, a dreamer, i be.

And so, dream away with my words for a spirit of me will be lit by the smiles or tears you feel, if any, while sharing these words from me to any eyes alive on planet blue.

Pause

To freeze is as is a drop of rain can fall from a cloud
As it continues to fall in release from pressure built within,
And drastic changes through the atmosphere as it comes nearer
It unfolds the memorizing abilities to transform from liquid to yes,
Frozen droplets to collect and cover the land as to last in its form
For extended time still to come.

As this drop does change from rain to snow, or ice even, before it falls to the ground below;
The earth in ground as well changes form to receive the snow yearly as leaves breathe last life
Grass begins to grasp last glory and fun from the sun before harboring itself until it can be freed again.

Before that water is captured in time as that freeze happens, there;
Right there, all the way cascaded in the high altitudes of the air,
The magic is of one we hardly ever see in natural eye sight,
Though it happens every season.

To be that drop and to take new form,
Is of a caterpillar does to be a butterfly after dreaming tight.

Realizations of ritualistically natural transformations
that are a true regulatiry.
Beauty is beheld and bestowed to nature and thus the
further built apart we grow different,
The planet will win at the end.

To change, change must be normalized in form of
expecting otherwise chaos can swallow whole.

Karma Smiles

Hello and goodbyes
Good mornings and goodnights.

Living until we die
Breathing throughout life.

As ecstasy is in mind
A feeling to grasp.

Much of paths chosen
Are often left before fully unfolded.

To fulfill is the dopamine of success
As is the completion of believing within the
within.

To win is to lose as a sorrow arrow may repent
but can not recurve aimers curve.
Leading to point of our paths guidance is ours to
pave or follow.

Begin or borrow is both a choice true to choose
Fear the voice you could lose if you decide to let
all choices pass as what freezes is the half empty

For the half full glass continues always but to the true believers who have concept in mind Over matter. The chakras all do align if inside we grasp the energies of which surround our lives.

Peace in the Morning

Living isn't easy. We all learn this lesson.

Some make the most with the least.
While some with the most give the least.

All boiling down to understanding values and worth.
If our lives were really equal from birth, no wars would ever have erupted.

Accept that we are the cause of our own pain.

Whether that hand of pain was passed down through time or not, one thing I see missing here:

Where are the people who know better?
Where are the people, like me;
Who have been by everyone in their lives' side as a spare shoulder to keep them together because we know and value we are all nothing if we stand by while another falls apart.

When are more going to stand up and say that the lived through the muddy rivers and rock slides life through their way, and by their own natural body instinct and resources, managed to survive.

Yes, many are thriving still. But as well, so many more are crying. Dying. Starving. Hurting.

We seem as a community okay with nonchalantly letting this all continue.

There's nothing we can do.
It's not in my control.
There's no order.

All the biggest complaints and all we wish is this simple system to lay itself on the line for us like our past generations did for it.

Did we not declare ourselves as a society of people to that of which was independent and has right to so govern themselves?

Why is there so much corruption that eye to eye I can't truly tell if a glare is well wished with concern or a death note for me behind my next turn?

No day will there be peace until we can thank the planet, the faces, the plants and animals all together for providing us, protecting us and sheltering us our whole lives while we degrade them more slowly over time.

Life is torture. Earth is not a playground. It is a battlefield.
The choice is ours if that's what is shall remain as.

Personally, I never heard the stories of the garden of eden, but I can only dream of living at least with a world where help was payment. Where kindness and a smile or laughter are a tip.

A penny was the price for a thought a century or more ago. Relentless have times become for gas skyrocketed and jobs took stress tolls.

Roads have been driving crumbling hands down our pockets for spare change and adding up it seems to overflow the surplus of expenditures needed.

When do the people get back for what they put in? We need that Thanksgiving to Remember.

We need to appreciate everyone around the table.

If we can't, we have no right to be spreading our negative energy.

To Poor Tales of Time Spent Unkind

To poor tales of times spent unkind…

Suicide of my dreams
Alone at nights, wrapped
Drowning in my screams.

Reality is lies
Fed to us like how
Crap is nasal porn
To a passing fly.

BETTING FOR BETTER?

Corruption will neigh let
The bug beat out any
Honest words for their
Tongues are sealed by a
Purely green paper deal.

Luckily for them
Suffering is of vast
Unknown for past
Down the line is misery.

Hard to imagine now
The desire to perspire.

Who's heart once filled
Brim to brim
Constantly overflowing
As such the opposite
Of a leaky bathtub.

The soul, so kind
Giving in and closed inside.

Cries mainly yelped
Now from internally.

To continue any pointless
Struggle with effort and
Strength fleeting fast

Hope that fart is
My last. Damn!
Smells all the way
Out the back.

Dial tone… wished for
A nicer tone.
Impress me first, or
First become last.

Water half empty
Or opportunity to
Realize all yet to
Loose is only what
Is still there with you.

To regrets, a plenty.

Must say finally…

I feel so lost.

Help could find me
Frozen in frost.

At that point,
Point is gone
And time moves on.

Remembering when the
World had a piece of a
Plan or a purposeful pen.

Too many times,
Lied to by invisible
Ties from these "BIG"
Corrupt company charge barges.

Hate to try to sleep
Memories like theirs
Haunting my dreams.

If you live life
Unafraid of the faces
Each day…
Maybe. . .
MAYBE……
We can all win.

As comforting
With: kindness, caring
Compassion and understanding.

Maybe… a new planetary
Chapter may begin?

Couldn't life just be
For happy and
Pleasant living.

Please…
QUIT THE RACE!
THERE IS NO NEED.

With over eight billion
On planet we reside on

How or why does any
One truly believe or
Aspire to be 'BEST' or
'FIRST'?! When I ask
If ever…..

Together? Work, solve,
Create and better evolve.

I don't want our races
Future books to be further
Disgraced by negligent
Intolerance and blatant
Disrespect.

My wish to fix
The confusion and put
An end to the disruption
Of chaos that soon, fears,
Swallows the minds of
Society in totalitarianism…
Finally…. They win.

If our lives are not
To be changed,
Then surely, go ahead.
Loose your mind by
"your choice"

Chip link for my brain?
Never have to self-think again?
Thank doctor billionaire.

Captive is the mind when control is nothing we care to bring along from our personal experiences.
A fish is only as fast as it's bubbling buoyancy will thus allow for them.

All aspects play developmental roles.

A message too true to speak as sands bordering a beach. To live and act as you wish all to be. Would we believe anything could be that easy.

A penny into the piggy bank.
Remembering times as a kid?

If the value of the penny were still the resonant equal
joy in monumental tone, could that be the beginning
to understanding?

As far as a planet can see, does one believe
How a nerve can send signals of disservice.

Ahh, the live of servitude.

To time: as it should be spent.
To you, this, one must decide the worth alone.

A planet of species,
Entirely in a misguided race.

Where do we really want to go off in space?

Time here may as well be replaced if we
Wage war as a bully breed mistakes.

If sea was comforting to see.
If an oyster was cherished with nutriment
To nourish and encourage that growth in
Treasure as time and energy spent.

To appreciating more of life in the natural outdoors.

And to my re-confirmed motto..

Kill them… With Kindness.
Guide them…. With kindness.

Lead them. . . With Kindness
Heal them. . . . W t K n n s .
Disturb them… with kindness
Cherish them. With KindNess.
Meet them… WITH kindness.
Feed them… with KINDness.
Hold them. . . With kindnesS.
Teach them. . . . .With KindNess.
LOVE THEM. . . WITH KINDNESS.
Dis-approve in them… w-i-t-h- -K-i-n-d-n-e-s-s-.
Time them… w..ith…kin.d.n.e.s.s..
Remind them.. with kind ness…
Destroy them… with kindness
Nurture them. . . With KINDness.
Help them. . . wItH kInDnEsS.

With Kindness!
WITH KINDNESS!
Apologies not needed….
        ….but appreciated!
Smiles…. Lend desires…..
        …. To explore more miles!
Spare…. Time to care…?
        . . . help isn't always there when needed.

Positivity is the best medicine,
Thus of which, MONEY
CAN NEVER SUPPLY FOR ANYONE!

The choice is yours.
Very few are destined for greatness.
Be a great you.

Keeping it simple stupid is as well if items aren't broken, why attempt any upgrades until problems slow current tasks.

There is always more than one way to arrive at similar outcomes or destinations.
Each step is a choice and life is a journey.

To the never-ending passions to constantly stay learning.
To beliefs that matter to you and that were all that mattered.

If we really took a moment to ask;
Why try to govern so many people by one base
Manu structure and guidelines,
Only is it a matter of time
Until the history pages repeat themselves.

Reform the rules we formed.
Destroy that of which are null and void
To start an era in time
Where sense is clear to see.
When we all take care of ourself,
Others and all life in equal aspects.

TO LIFE:
All was and will continue to be and become from the minds.

Start of all our time:
initially created by one super being's dreams in thoughts.

Continuance of our time:
Help is possible but confusion and delusion muddy the streams of happiness to bliss.

Futures of our times:
the main being foresees and we live masked lives of misery. To prosper or advance with any positive chance, internalize ourselves before any further plans or actions for judgement lead to failures.
Life is what we make it. Dreaming to see all happy.

Fish lake planted in middle of ground where upper north be.

Some words are utterly nonsense in all forms of the terminology of the word.

As service in these days lacks on many verbs and leads to dissatisfactory tones.

Service with a smil-
E. Gosh, feels like it's been since F-
Riendly's days when families rode in
Vans to enjoy a dependable
Ice cream as a happy ending
Cone and it may have Fudg-
E drizzled on the whipped cream ripples.

I don't see why this world is acting outraged.
All the faces we most often aggravate while we let
Out the inner rage we accepted and had locked,
forced down inside.

Like unlocking your phone to bring out the jams
Pandora can
Spread throughout the air to bring pleasure to our
ears.
As easy as opening those cardboard boxes all our
Endless purchases show up packaged in.

Time's always on the same plane, never to our
surprise.
When we agree that we annoy one another with
Undivided disrespect. We all hate everyone but
ourselves.
Deep down… tell me that's not true?

Look at life through your eyes and make your
Path in your own footprints. Worry about what you
Can control, for opening those doors to others to
Expect understanding and empathy is entirely
Ignorant. Sharing personal views is almost
Always doomed to negative results.

Similarities and necessities is the basics
Of holding our society and dispersing
Further mind wondering as confused by
Another's views that neither correlated or
Felt related. Insecure is a phase until
It becomes the gemstone of our foundation.

Alpha-Poem-Bits

A to the B
And don't forget how to C.
Staffed by D and ruled by thriving E's in owned minds,
All F can do is praise G whilst
Self-pleasing with HI smooshed together
Wondering why J flew when K was a tod.
L was hard to the streets with M who none should hope
To meet for N was the trained O before
P came along and got Q turned
Into a whole new R and dissolved all accords held by S.
T never knew anything for blinded by U was T.
V was blowing off fumes wishing W had left
The details Y would have needed to find X in the correct
Location for Z is always the least help as hidden as the
end fortails.

Words Mean Nothing

How much more negativity can our whole society dish and
forget like it was nothing they could have said?
How long can we continue to harshen our own winters with our
cold actions and thoughtless responses?

People far as eye to eye can see, as our future or our demise.

When will we open up to the realization that our words mean
nothing when emotions are kept out of what we say?

Electronics are the main cause of this.

How much worry did past generations truly endure?

I truly can't compare the past times to current.

As I wish everyone else would realize the same.

We are all here whether we like that or not.
Poverty is not a one way melting pot. Do we not all see this?

If one person, or one community, is suffering.

How strong are we entirely as a divided planet then?

If there were to ever be an external force whose desire were
ever to be to wipe humans off this earth;

Do we stand a chance if we are continuing to self-divide ourselves?

When will standing up for right become the new age of just living life true as true?

Number one is nothing if we are pointing it in other's faces. Just makes the bragger seem conceited.

Big actions and hearts in hand need to lead the way to brighter days.

If we keep up this way, how do you expect to enjoy stars at night when years down the road all our stars are gone by the light we can't hide inside our solar zone because our nights are now internally as bright as day is to us from externally.

Soon, we won't even have any words that can come to a mutual comprehending in any understanding for our abilities to relate to one another will fade all mainly due to us as a group just taking in on the death toll that I stare at called a phone…

Phone home not many of us do though.

It's convenience this.
All of it. Believe it caused destruction in our world wide tomb.

When our words mean nothing… what else could that refer to?
When we speak our words and languages no more, that's the fate of our times.

Bottles and plates, each to enjoy and share words of thoughts.

Penny was the worth for a thought back in the old days.

Now, a thought could go for a new dollar in worth for no value could be placed on realness anymore.

Our society is hiding behind faces of makeup,
Behind bars our government claims will help criminals repent and learn their lessons,
But what will we ever learn if each time we teach by closing doors?

Help is extending yourself when you have nothing more inside and all internally you are pulling apart.

Discomfort in new experiences is how we develop and grow through new understandings.

How does any further forms of blossoming hope to ensue if there is no one persistent enough to desire better from others as a community anymore?

Years behind in past now has come to us as a dream or a nightmare.

Would anything be different if we had made one move otherwise?

No. where one actions happens, another will always correlate to equilize.

View the Sap Day

Down went the red blood as it fell as sap drips from the noble maple tree providing a sticky syrup of protection; thus blood loss was of same matters for blood from drops of cried tears is a force of natural effects for balance. This has been proven time and again, as age old stories will behold.

The bill of war is a course for thieves and beggars, but who is not a wonderer of truths and wisdom of life. As forth the values of which so many seek, vast fortunes and glorious wonders; doom shall be the only comfort as they wish now for sleep when they spat out the humble pie and defecated on the moral juices of honor and dignity.

We are the time when men and women are so unique that our minds have gone mad with loose laws and narrow guidance.

As I was told, loose lips sink ships. Snitches get stitches. Speak only when what you have to say is of value to your company you keep.

I believe I speak to all as one company of people if we can agree on one thing. We are all different. But we are at the same time, all the same.

Who does not require to eat of nourish their body? Who knows the memories of which the embers in the cells maintain?

We are as much life as we are death. We do not ever remember the beginning or the end, as far as the dash in the middle, what we make of this is our choices as our lives grow forward in time.

Washing away with rain from a storm so full of pressure that not only does water cry into the streets in flowing streams of force, thunder screaming and lightning striking with fury and sparking every dry weathered bough that lay down it's path.

This is the way in a matter of analogies that would be comparative to the war we rage upon our own kind across lands.

How are we ever going to improve our lives as a whole if we can't step back before we send all of us to our personal planks to walk.

Positive Viewing

As we grow older and age through time, moving slows with each new step.
As the saying goes, either to use your body or lose it.
More to be added to the saying lists:
Keep it simple stupid.
If we all were to lose track of what in which we physically have the control over and what we mentally crave to control but in which we can never do is when madness turns to consume our soul.

So, to grow old in a world where once, mean words were kept by holding tongue and anger was settled with bullets shot out from barrels of our guns;

When all of the fighting from war is done, the sun rises to us again and lives that were living and livid before may now be those whose souls lost to the fight. May they finally rest in peace.
What was the fight for? In the end, is there any reason we need to continue to be a world where words are not enough?
How far away is the silent treatment?
If that means peace treaty or human extinction, either is possible.

Plausible to say, that views and words are so easily construed when interpreted from one mind to the next as there may be many hidden languages of meaning to a person's sentence.

All of life in which one person experiences, is never comparable to another souls outlook post life's experience.

This to me holds the key to why I both love and despise the expression of asking another to try to "walk in another's shoes."
This is entirely impossible as we look at one life as every day to day aspect and we realize that each person to person interaction, each meal, every breath, all steps taken or not and down to each blink of our eyes.

No way is it ever going to be possible to fully emphasize the experience of another person's life through their personal views.

As this would lead a conclusion that seems that personally, we are a unique ecosystem of the most extreme type of life form where we are all atomically individual walls with each their own set frame of working or shutting down.

Their set ups are all close in main stem in design. But to compare is not possible from one mind to the next as the exact same feeling that understands the exact stem of a single memory, view or thought can create.

So relate or negate, choose to be happy at least..

If I were to be in the views to needing anything in my life for basics, two main things I live on every day:

Coffee and positivity.

I have my own superpower, I could call it. Freedom of speech. Whatever.

Having the profound ability to perceive every single activity or event and finding the hole of light.

Turning darkness into lightness is a huge string of holding my soul's fiber intact.

So much so that all of my cooking, artworks or writing. Any of my animal loving's, video game time or nature adventures.
None is so enjoyable if not in a positive state of mind.

And so for any current position to turn negative to .....

Poetic Justice League

In a world run by monkeys,
Under water bubblers a plenty.

World full of empty words,
With chaos filling every verse.

Here we sit, many lonely hearted,
Laughing in our own fumes of close sharts
Fully loaded by blaster farts
Fueled by fast food drive through cycles.

Words may not claim tolls in lives;
Maybe not in the way we see to realize.

Before we close our minds to far,
And before any bridges burn or rivers barred…

How is a life behind bars?
Cold.
How is a life with opinions forced on hold?
Cold.
How is it to dream of a world with happy faces because past conflicts are placed where they should have been left in the first place…so dreaming of a reality that feels pointless and effortless to even imagine a potential realism is always going to leave anyone feeling…
COLD.

Cold and alone is the resonant tone that I feel from Earth.

Did this happen as a curse?
Will we be able to reverse our deeds and right whatever may need?

Our existence, none was offered. There has never been a baby who had the choice to voice their vote within the tomb to be birthed or blast from the womb in an operating room.

The sooner we all come to realize that the world will never provide for all of us until we all learn to stop denying one another in times of need or when an occurrence of nature has left a storm we trouble to weather through.

Whatever circumstances lead to tell; one thing needs to be a certainty.

For life to further evolving, prospering or even have a mutual forthcoming tone of respect to lay down future steppingstones for minds to continue the ever-fluctuating needs of separating rights and ideals.

State-government-church-school-town-city-person-pet

We are all a united and brokenly divided community.

The television. The reporters. The deciders of fates that lead us to becoming rivals.

A river will not freeze its flow to stop short.

Nor will a roaring fire blow itself to embers.

To the point of these I am making is that life will not pause for us.

Life will never yield to our demands.

We have control of what we realize we have control over.

As to push a mountain down to rubble to clear for the clouds passing by would be a fore passable action that most could never fashion to even imagine.

May come to be because to this day, this is an unrealistic idea to even contemplate for any reason.

Point was there though to show that imagining the impossible,
Yes, like in a wonderland of no real ideas where all the best ideas are only the crazy ideas.
We all like to forget the childish mind state of being naive and believing in something just because it's fun to play make believe.

Bring back your child's heart.

Bring back the joy you had as a kid.

Now no one has a perfect life.

Let me clear that.

So, stop comparing yourself or anyone else to, well, anybody else.

We are all only human and all only given one chance.

Make it count or stop wasting others time.
Do what you can today. Don't overdo though for a day can only fit as much as any itinerary can hold without unfolding itself to appearing too bold.

Weathering any storm when it's just too cold outside,
Is often simply best to come back inside.

Staying safe and keeping things simple is the key to a life of simple happiness.

Halos are for protective souls who have life and passion and care for all time bestowed.

To this day, and to each ahead,

Living life one step at a time.
Stepping on my right foot and not forgetting,
Is how I plan to breathe through each struggle of any new day or fun game yet to be

Champ

What does it mean to be alive?
What is the reason to mortality and the point to virtues?
Why is the ability to decide in one mind not an attribute that is more shared with common viewed local communities?
Why is war and hate forever seeming to be a major contemplation that withstands so far that a vacation is impossible for most due to times that are currently crooked by misconstrued views from past locks we just will not release our begrudging from.

For a nightly masquerade of plays from faces which are more worthless than a fall leaf soaked from burnt embers and veins to which will strongly remember the storms it has such withered through.

As such, nature, world, life. All equivocal to the representation of which we all have similar essential needs to the recipe to not one survival, but total survival.

Say times to which we are viewing as our future to be true, and we are planning and working not only ourselves too hard, but sourcing our planet, our home, and its soul resources as well.

When will enough become the views, we finally see?

The generations handing down their opinions. Creation of onions.
So forward as to claim thus as well creates monsters. Beasts.
Incapable life forms of even the title of human for a family that passes everything down through every new generation from the dime to the time, the memories, and all recipes. This form of social diplomacy and bureaucracy is corruption of all humanity's proper efforts over the thousands of years of cultural growth and as professionally research and development to creating and worthwhile planet for all to comfortably live on.

The ability to reform the downslope of a planets failing environment and all biological aspects of which are so essential to the proper functionality of the health of this home of Earth.

To a doomed fight we wonder years continuously asking, ourselves, why we enlisted and trained and compiled as a united entity to do what we still internally resist to be complied to do. Are we so inclined to fight, to build our hate weapons from our resources, and to charge fuel and explode our own souls?

Whether we agree on this or not, one this we all must accept.

Divided we fall. Together we fly.

As saying the point is that we are all on one planet. Included and enclosed in one solar system.

We are all in this for ourselves. For if one succeeds. Realize that we celebrate because we all succeed in this.
So far to say, that everything has more value than we realize.
One of the opposites is true in a monumental way as well. We create waste. Massive and excessive amounts of waste.

Products that are "decorations" and such are collecting dust forever.

Hoarding is a problem and not a good one.
Filth is all around us. The wealth of a business. Or a state. Or any party needs a limit.

The planet will never be able to prosper as much as it should be able to in mere realistic views.

But the certainty is that change is a bill that needs a passing check in all boxes.

In the clearest explanation, all need an evaluation and then a change and of most productive and empowering as seen fit for each respective scenario.

The most effective way to create a world filled with happy people who have desires to be pleasant and follow the rules as one to survive and thrive as one; it is easiest to keep it simple.

So today this would realistically mean a total change in all structures.

Best way to do this quickest and most informatively is to wipeout.

Like a tv show grabs the attention for its personal ratings and development.

We need a society wipeout of all in place rules and guidelines.
Of all set wages and time bars.
We need to clarify all we know to a public knowledge so that nobody must wonder ever.

If we can come to stop hiding our faces like we smudged our makeup and cannot even realize the book, we shamefully sit behind is upside down.

Ridiculous is how we should all be feeling for a world of hate. No sin is of value to waste extra time to sin more to cover pain from a first sin.

Revenge will never comfort loss.

And vengeance fueling anger and disrespect with no purpose will forever be a pointless effort.

Time has supplied everything we need.
And human greed is slowly diminishing that supply more over time.

When it comes to late and it is close to gone, that is when an Ark from Noah could not even save us.

We have souls.
We have looked too long to conquest all with fear.
We fear ourselves most. As all the entire solar system imaginably does or could as well.

But to saying: "Everybody deserves a second chance." And "Change is possible if you provide enough resilient continuous effort to the trial-and-error stages to get to a point of understanding the source of issue to start to view the bigger picture."

If all is well that ends well, and nothing is fair in love and war, then how far will we push our own planets geotechnic plates apart?

We are one in heart.
Is it time to enable ourselves as a caring entity?

Caring for our planet wide community.
Caring for preserving and even reviving our planet.
As well, caring for just being a non-problematic biological force withing this solar system we are within.

No one being will ever be able to hold all the answers that the scroll of explanations and knowledge, the reasoning of power and time, and weight as towards mass. To knowing the collateral scale of which our solar system lives suspended, revolving and spiraling in would be of an overwhelming and expansive passing of nervons and an explosion of growth within membrane processing compacities.

Poetic Truth is Still in Pain

Today in America and all over the world, people are bowing to their governments.

We, and by we I refer to the general population who are supposed to be represented, are actually being fooled by our own government and taken advantage of.

I feel we are leading into a new era of possible tyranny and dictatorship.

Times are looking grim.

I have never believed in any of these ‘conspiracy theories’, but now, I see no way that can explain everything going on in this world that seems “unjust” or “unfair” or just plain “detrimental to the welfare of the population”.

For example, take for instance the situation with the tobacco/nicotine industry.

We have known for YEARS!!! For no, for DECADES! That cigarettes have been killing people and in so many possible ways.

We continue to sell them, to promote them and to endorse them.

I have asked the question as to why for years.

I struggle with my nicotine addiction stemming from picking up smoking cigarettes at 16 years old.

I found vaping at 25 years old, about a year ago. It saved my life. I'm not kidding.

I hate seeing that we are trying to ban vaping. I don't even know where to begin with how messed up this situation is.

How is the government allowed to enact a ban for vaped and their flavored products that are saving people's lives with the claim that they are "thinking about the future of the children"?

This is the biggest load of steaming bull crap I have ever heard.

If they are going to argue that, and that the flavors are the problem, then how can you still sell candy-promoting obesities and diabetes and unhealthy lifestyles and diets, or what about alcohol-duis and impaired decisions and so many other complications.

How can you ban the one thing that actually has a good intent and purpose to in turn tell us that a resolution to not having our flavors, you're producing a vaping product that we are still required to buy the physical cigarettes, attach them to the device and vape the cigarettes through your fda approved device?

You there in your high seat in your chair sitting there making these decisions behind our backs and not giving the public their own options to decide for themselves what they need to feel better?

I used cigarettes to feel better at times, and it helped me when I was using them.

You don't understand the dependency you build literally THE INSTANT you light that very first cigarette. I know. I can tell you it's not easy to deal with.

That's why I've been infuriated by them just completely and unjustly taking away all options for me to have access to my vape.

Due to this, and the bad impressions that the government has implemented on the entire crowd of vapers, I have had no choice than to purchase a pack of cigarettes from time to time.

After one pack I can't breath. After one cigarette I need another. I get shifting and shady when looking at that pack. It's an addiction that will kill me if I continue it. I am not given an option that will help me continue to feel the relief I need to feel without the complications from the problem.

I want to also just add that the argument that they are using as well that the weed vaped are bad too, let me explain how I see this as well.

I have never been an avid smoker most of my life.

Back in 2018 I got a medical card because I realized that using different forms, different strains, different dosages can yield different effects and provide relief from a wide range of varying symptoms.

I have been a regular smoker since early 2019. In late 2019 I had a vape that I had a very stupid moment and without doing my own proper research I refilled that empty vape cartridge with something I soon found out was very harmful and painful.

That product was a hemp based mainly topical or edible liquid which I found out contains vitamin E.

This is what is harmful. Vitamin e.

And physical cigarettes.

There is so much more I can say.

Let me end my rant by advising every single person who made it this far to go do some research on the topic.

Here are some informative starter links:

https://www.tobaccofreekids.org/assets/factsheets/0365.pdf

https://www.tobaccofreekids.org/assets/factsheets/0365.pdf

If you wanna see the most messed up parts in that second link, make sure you notice that all numbers are representing millions of dollars and look at the column all the way to the right where the money was solely intended to be used to provide the general with options to prevent nicotine addiction. Look at all the glorification the cigarette companies get instead though!? The publicity and advertising and promoting from so many entities.... Everyone's sold their soul to the fat cat in charge of the nation

America-Z

America, the beautiful.
Built by the backbones of the brave.
Countries as a unity.
Divine nature, abundance of resources.
Equality; the eternal and everlasting dream.
Fears are of unaware hatred.
Grievance is as worn times approach.
How does freedom become of an
Independent right, privilege and
Justified precedence through society?
Kindness has a firmness
Like no anger could truly conquer.
Memories fade as true as time in
Now has now already become the past.
Offended or offering? Choose your
Path wisely for karma can be
Quick to teach as well as
Rocks can break bones.
Slowly, war machines decrease.
Tanks of yesterday are now
Used as percussion instruments of
Variable tones and musical
Waves of acoustic frequencies.
Xenobiotic flood is of Halo fears.
Yankee union or federal rebels?
Zwitterion would be a hermaphrodite ion.

Life, Love and Lessons with Will Wik Wallrace

Love is but an egg in fragility, though as well being as a flower in vibrance.
The sacred heart is but an empty black hole of icy solitude until a match opens barriers, we lock tight.
A dragon ignites flames across lands but loving a beauty for inside smiles with, that's when your life becomes full.
As one unite of life continues, more will always follow to consume what was before. Survival of the fittest.

Children grow up and learn not just from teachers, but life, as life is but it's own best lesson guide.

Instances will prove times of faith or those we vote to accept but now knowing the true color of their sleeves is all a continues mislead tangled mess of twine stitched with so much haste even elmer would wish to shield his face from the shambled souls.

What is truly a shame to see as a regular in life is the ignorance and the shade.

For a need as one has to live happy and survive, who is any to strike one of this joy?

Money does not grow on trees they all told us.

Man, we are so stupid if we don't realize it's doom that money will lead us all straight towards.

The more trees we create pointless endebting bills,
Now I know as I see with my eyes.
Nothing matters, no one matters and nothing is equal to cash when it talks.

Is money nice to be alone with?
Will money ever share anything with us?

Short answer. No.
Not anymore. Before our saws or axes chopped down the barking trees to fund our cravings for currency, and only before would it have had any true value to us.

We seem to be forgetting the needs everyone shares of oxygen and sunlight, clean water and an assortment of fresh foods.

What nobody needs are houses filled by hoarders.
Could be use for homeless or emergency shelter boardings.

What we need to forget is the feeling of helplessness. And what is the number one insecure trait built into our emotional reaction system? Failures to succeed.

What is success though?
That means many different things to many different people.

What it should only mean is you are still breathing right now. So you are still succeeding no matter what at life.

When we destroy our outlets for air production, trees, or shade to rest out from a hot sun. we will decline into the dark times of peril.

No more should our massive failing buildings haunt our streets or cities.
No more should the dead fill our useable lands. No more should we bury the dead for we know the waste it causes and the dead deserve total peace and rest. They will not get that under dirt as a box of rotting bones and flesh.
The worms crawl in
The worms crawl out
First your stomach and
Then out your eyes and mouth.
They eat your nose
And the jelly between your toes.
So don't you ever laugh
As a hearse goes by;
For you never know
If you may be the next
To die.

Meows are a melody and life is not such a mystery. What we tend to do too often is complicate what is often already solved.

Answers are often right in front of us. All just a question away. So wondering and pondering is fine when planning for words to find, but saving squabbles from nonsense may be harder than appears for clear to see eye to eye is not always easy to share to hold as in hand in hand of true deep understanding of the explicit point of view.

A building is only as tall as one feels. For if a mountain has a view so extreme but the height is not much of vast extremes, but the journey is dangerous and challenging, struggles ahead and proper equipment needs to be readily of hand to reach that promise land view…
Or the choice of number two…
The sky scraper that you can pay that arm and leg and energy from the journey to take stairs, or, if lucky a very long ride up an elevator to a room or roof that touches over other buildings to open a new view into the realms of which reality outside exists.

Which door appeals to more is an ethical question.
As well would be if both doors should be accessible to all who wish.

Many questions are still out there filling many minds and many may never find an answer they feel fits their specific question.

And to that night moon, and to the morning sun.
The rain clouds and the brisk wind.
The plants, insects, mammals and reptiles.
The birds of many feathers and the amphibians as well.
As a sparrow sings in solace,
What wind washed wet Wik Will Wallrace out west was way windier when whipping Wik Will Wallrace whimpering wound a wet wooshing winter window in Willowfyre where Wik Will Wallace was once from.
Nonsense will remain longer than we should ever hope.

Whamm

Opposition-attraction
Dedication-frustration
Learning-loosing
Loving-using
Choosing-wasting

Every step is a celebration.
How many steps do you take each day?
How many babies take their first step each day?
How many cats' steps are there each day for more paws they have to cross the floor with each way they step.

Forgiveness is willingness to accept.
Not necessarily to give in as to forget.

Realizing that showing mercy or remorse is sometimes the best way to plan a steady course.

Teaching a lesson does not always need to require any retaliation or force of torture or harm.

Sometimes the best way to teach someone what they do is wrong is to walk them through how to do things in multiple other ways and let them choose a way that is best for them and disrupts least as well.

Love is a teacher as well.

For no greater teaching can one feel from the pride of a role model that they have viewed as a guider or a mentor.
Need no teaching degree to make a difference in someone's life and possibly help them turn away from a dark and dusty trail to maybe even weeding out their own new path and then clearing the way and nurturing it for others to follow in a brighter walkway to the future of possibilities.

We create all.
We destroy all.
We love all.
We hate all.
We all have the same sets of abilities.
Even the neighboring plants and animals we live and exist with.
We all eat, rehydrate, require sun and oxygen.

Yes, some species have various oddities that make some resilient to the needs of these sources.

Nonetheless, we need to take responsibility some day to plan for the future and realize that no matter how awesome a car may be, or how awesome a plane or tank can seem. A train or a boat. We need evaluations of what we really are doing with these forms of transit to the planet.

Yes, we can get around faster and freely than the old days.

Are there any other options?

Say teleportation rather than transportation.

Regardless of anything else. We all can hear the news and should be able to use some form of common sense to conclude that the smog, that the oil, that the waste dumping and nuclear and extended wars have undisputedly caused our planet too reclusively become overly polluted by toxication to the wellbeing of the support of our planet.

And to go as far forward as to be against free will and rights to ban abortions still.
How stone aged could anyone ever be?
Our planet is so far overpopulated already.
People should get a medal for getting an abortion these days.

Truly suggesting that abortions be medically funded and scientifically studied and researched more and even more so, for the reason that some day we may be our only hopes to feed and supply for ourselves.

Is it too crazy to imagine that if any danger for civilization were to present itself and foreseeable animals became hard to come across, who's to disagree that if there were more doctors who had been researching and performing abortions and the nutrients and test were able to verify any uses for such fetuses other than their lives that were not brought into this world.

Who's to say that a person who is carrying an infant, maybe that infant is the ticking time bomb to society because they carry a disease that will kill everyone.

Whose to say that if that fetus were not aborted, we could even be having any discussion about it right now or ever?

And to research that unborn human further after removal could prove medically sufficient at providing possible cures or who knows what could be discovered.

But if someone wanted to or needed to have an abortion, in these days, or ever, who is there who is in the right to say no to someone making their own decision.
Peace resolves perceptions.

In a World

In a world where our each and every turn,
We often forget to question whose to gain or lose
From each action we make or choose.

So, for many hunger is a norm,
As awful for them to know,
That tables nearby are wasting bits
And whole carcasses just for safety's sake.

Being fair is not easy when all our lives
Life is always at war.

This is what makes us stronger
If we look into how to develops bonds better.

People are a race of species.
Benevolent and mysterious as far
Superior and inferior.

Opposites that attract also tear our inner seams.

When we remember the trickling tone of a stream,
Or the guitar strum or beat down on a drum.

What makes the world happy is when we all have our
space.

Space is vast and wide, and circles or squares cannot hide.

What can be hidden is self.
Thus, the meaning of selfish and selfless.

To be one and to be the other is both one and the same.

To be a helping and caring being is to be one who lives to be the best self they can see for the world around them to be at least disturbance and most hope for peace.

This is the way we wish to spread sweet dreams.
Is it not?

I can not imagine a world where:
If there are no hungry bellies at night;
If there is no jealousy or reason to fight.
If there was no need to hurt another.
More.
No worries of wars.
No worries to open your doors.
No worries of being forced to fight fights you didn't start.

Reasons for answers.

To believe in a time where all division of man and woman.
Or adult or child.

Of any person near or far.
If we open our knowledge from the past as a new way to a better tomorrow.

Is this an action I would approve of for today's people?

Yes. As I as well have questions from past views and reports that we may all wish answers found in our research.

As one must ask though.
The day-old question.

If answers were laid on the table, clear as can be and no other choice can change what may be done;

Will just the peace of knowing the true provide these same sweet dreams we may need?

Can closure be as closed as a book, and we hold no more anger or spread no more hate from just knowing may end our hearts ache?

At the end of the road, as we reach a bench near the bend of the tree encased lake with wind pushing crinkled leaves about the frosty summer air.

Reminiscent of the sunrises and sorrowful of lost sunsets as we often miss and lose those from interest.

Better issues need to be in mind when any one further goes to government or public time.

We hurt so many lives by "trying to teach them of their crimes;"
But really it should be more like:
"Hey, I'll make more money off you are being in prison and ruin your life forever so your dime is a never ending dollar fill up."

It's sad when lives are so clearly at such a loss for words that fakeness and rage or mistaken glances can end all further breathes or dancing chances.

Leftovers and sleepovers. Tumble weeds and dancing trees.

Horse back by the beach and a sudden stunning red fox running down the street.

Don't forget to smell the daisies and look around some more so you don't go crazy.

Love each step or you may make a big regret.

Life is more than dollar bills and a true smile will fill your pocket more and a hug can fill your house with bountiful warmth.

Blood is thicker than water.

Which is why I finally believe I understand the reason why Jesus may have made a metaphor in his action of turning said "Water into wine."

How divine would it be to say all of time that family holds us together?
As well that blood is thicker than water.
But the grapes of wrath they fill with ash
When water turns to wine.
Of family a bickering,
And time keeps flickering.
I wish to live with mere merriment
And let go of distribuend.

And so, the message I translate as I see it is that wine, may poison us.
And so may water.
It's all in the battle and knowing when to choose which for when you need to win or lose.

The cat's up on cloud nine are the one's whose bellies are almost never hungry for their whiskers would soon turn to mush or jelly.

Smell the flowers some extra before you take your next bend.
Catch your own fish to fry as a Sunday surprise.

The time you spend will only make you as happy as you equivalate the probability of happiness out to be.

Thus, is how the simplest things in life are often just undeniable the greatest.

Like a giant steaming fresh plate of home cooked perfectly fluffy and moist cracked with pure and tender love and care.
Yes! Scrambled eggs of course!
And the best side to any plate of eggs, besides some cheese on top,
Is a whole pile of bacon nearby.
And whoever doesn't just love popping their bacon into their microwave for shear convenience and easy bacon pleasure: You're straight lying to yourself in my eyes.
But a home cooked meal can brighten any mood and lift about any negative spirit.

So stars will always seem bright when the night has gone darkest.
And the sun rise will always rise from the east and west to it's sleep.

And the 365.25 days our revolving ball of blue and brown a green gloop takes to make another full cycle;
All with a whole other group of planets and other eco and solar systems known and unknown so far to exist.

What a crazy and beautiful gift we all have of life on this planet.

Are we going to waste one more second fighting or wasting time, resources, energy, or money?

For what reason? Pride? Respect? Bragging rights?
I want to brag when we are all at a state of time when no one around the planet is struggling.
When no where is there any more hatred being spread by past negligent parties actions.
Turning the keys to each person's destiny is not easy and not every one will always fulfill their destiny.

We make our life how we can and not every step is up to our control.
As well, many other factors take a toll or help our growth in our time from embryo, to infancy, child, adolescent, young adult, middle aged, golden aged and finally elderly.

There is no set span that all these stages of life will line up for along any group of people.

Therefore the best we can really do, and are doing, is making charts. Taking data.
With most accurate and detailed information, the graphs could show a whole new blend of pie we may not ever have realized was possible but was in the oven the whole time.

Who truly knows is who searches endlessly for the answers of which their questions do lead them towards?

Follow the yellow brick road?
Red pill or blue pill?
Did you see where that rabbit went?

All time and time was will ever more be merely a memory.
Life is and isn't as it seems; why else would so many question if it were all just a dream?
DOROTHY! DOROTHY! Just keep Toto locked up and we'll all be alright.

Deport or Teleport?

Teleportation is more possible than deportation.

We just don't realize the equivalent equation between making the relation between point A. and point B. relevant in which to pass an object through co-inconsequently.

To any matter of which this would be possible would need to rely on the plane and the axis as a specific destination.

Mapping the exact location in aspects of all dimensions in separate dimensional maps for each format.

From that point, the lay out of each point's geographical, agronomical and asperity is available for positioning the alignment of said new object.

Main issues being the mode of transporting then once the mapping of precious locations has been performed and checked for any discrepancies of error.

The most powerful form of transportation is by creating a force zone around said object with naturalized energy only.

Naturalized energy is anything non processed by man.

So to explain, this would include sound in vibrations and frequencies and tones of different variations. It would also be inclusive of wind energies in multidirectional vortexes as well as spiral wind tunnels and whirling whistles of strong thrusting gusts.

As well as the sound and wind energies, it will most definitely require solar energy as a main source of a base. The base is the main establishment that all objects will need to be transported from one to another. The base is in another term, a home plate or a mailbox.

There are other energies to harness as forces as strong as those mentioned previously but they require a much vaster supply of natural resources to fulfill the ability to prove useful. But as such, are a valuable noted mention as a resource still it be.

Plant’s photosynthesis is an attractant to capture and release and forming a new. So rebirth and growth and life is in each leaf and stem and the stronger the seed’s roots grow, the mightier the use of the plant’s abilities.

Lastly and certainly not least is heat and other natural geo energies.

Such include molten lava, magnetic attraction and repulsion, magnitude of motion powerful in force to shake tectonic plates to differentiating degrees of severity.

There are certainly other things I have left unmentioned as of yet to include in this memento. For another time. Soon.

Keep it Saucy for Me

Sauce

For a flavor, or a taste.
For desire not on hold.
The spread wished smoothed on even.
Any cheese or toppings simply pleasing.

For a pizza, tomato and cheese.
Easy to please with mozzarella and cheddar.
Hard to perfect a buffalo chicken,
Perfect crust with bubbles a must.
The sauce, like a boss,
Best coming off any pizza line,
Is deserving of a buffalo sauce basis.

Next level has the chicken,
My taste prefers that gold.
Crispy fried tender strips.
Chopped and sauced with even more.
Buffalo dreams galore.

There's where the cheese tops
With all perfect mix of mozzarella and cheddar.
No better way to design a buffalo pizza
That could please all lovers of a good burn you just
can't put down with all flavors in every layer.

Monster

Inside

Alive

Cats at night.

Silently sleeping by our sides.

Red rum. Murderers in their run.

Nature's killer instinct in a one claw paw.

Faster than any whisker and pounce.

Catchers of the mice and the pawers who play nice.

My bowl. Don't like to say twice. Meows. Purrlites

Dreams

Silently as we yell, though in our sleep screams don't travel well.
Fear consumed in mind plays tricks behind shut eyes.
Often in despair if sorrows are ever meaningfully realized.
A crow does not squawk to alert bystanders of any intentions.
In life, we all learn our lessons one day or another unless we decide to remain ignorant,
As for that, the lesson favorable to karma is loneliness.
Life is a blessing just as a hotdog can serve as a meal if chosen as just that.
On the other hand, that single same hot dog could be a feast and a celebration if chosen as so.
Our minds retain if not enhance connections while our bodies lay at rest, and though our eyes may close to the doors we can walk through, our mind can travel with less resistance from our legs.

Maybe Not Today…

If not tomorrow, today.
If not today, yesterday.
If not yesterday, then never.
Holding on to lost items, closes our hands and hearts to new blessings.
A mask of mud or makeup sweat through like sludge and all in and out of each day's end is rush and rage.
Does the madness ever end? What turn do we correct?
Wages added to wars and tolls pooling years and power fueling purses but where's our just desserts at? People every day are hungry around the world.
Fearing the curiosity of the infamous cat becoming the fate of an entire human race? I know I am.
To imagine the state of panic for political response.
To know of bills to protect and serve our people that not only are not fulfilled, neglected and for some unkindly reason, we have become victims to and of our government.

Peace In Woes

Dominos or dominoes?
Pizza or game?
Is there time to go back to explain?
Values are a full box deal.
As such of a full circle pizza.
Morals are lessons learned through time.
When mistakes happen and we can figure out how to reassemble wrongs as such to restack an early topple of some dominoes tiles, that's the challenge we all face.
Now without morals, one will never have a full set to understand the reasonings and ethics of virtues.
To be dealt your values is to select your toppings on your pizza. These values vary person to person as they are experience biased structures of lifetimes.
Gathering these values together with morals will create a prime example of a reasonable and conscious being.

www.ingramcontent.com/pod-product-compliance
Lightning Source LLC
Chambersburg PA
CBHW051735130826
49812CB00033B/865
9789357440387